Copyright © 2017 by PAUL F. BELARD

ALL RIGHTS RESERVED

ISBN: 978-0-9972726-9-7

Printed in the United States Of America
Linden Press
Greenlawn, New York 11740

Edition of 50 copies signed by the author.

Cover design by Paul Bélard
Cover set up by Walter Sargent, sargentwebservices. com

Paul Bélard

ELVIS

HAWAII, NOVEMBER 1957

Linden Press
Greenlawn, New York

Preface

At the end of October 1957, Elvis, Scotty Moore, Bill Black, D.J. Fontana and the Jordanaires had just completed a four-day tour of three cities that included San Francisco, Oakland and Los Angeles. The tour, which was initially scheduled to be the last one in 1957, was promoted by Lee Gordon. So why Hawaii? *Jailhouse Rock*, Elvis' third film, had opened nationally on November 8th and Elvis, when interviewed on his arrival, said that the shows in Hawaii were added as a result of a delay in the start of his next movie. In *Elvis Day by Day*, Peter Guralnick suggested that it quite possibly was at least influenced by the fact that the Colonel himself had been stationed in Hawaii during his brief Army career, between 1929 and 1932, and he took the opportunity to visit with old friends. An article in the *Honolulu Star Bulletin* on November 8, 1957 also gave this explanation:

21,000 Isle Christmas Cards in '56 Gave Elvis Idea to Sing Here Sunday

Elvis Presley's manager, Colonel Tom Parker, said today the biggest incentive for the rock 'n roll singer's appearance here were the 21,000 Christmas cards received from Hawaiian Island fans last year.
The gyrating Presley is scheduled to perform in two shows, 3 and 8:15 pm., Sunday in the Honolulu Stadium.
He arrives on the Matsonia scheduled to dock at 9 a.m., Saturday, and will probably take the next ship back to Los Angeles and on to Memphis, Tennessee, according to Parker.
"The boy, hates airplanes, I don't know why," he added.
He said the show was mapped out "in 30 minutes over lunch last Thursday" and Two days later he was here making arrangements.
Original plans for an Australian tour were canceled, "but we may change our minds at the last minute," he said.
Presley, who grosses $800,000 annually, will be assisted on stage by the Blue Moon Boys, a band combo; the Jordanaires quartet; and a variety troupe.
Parker, who has been managing the money-making Presley for more than two years, describes his charge as "a very popular kid—but real humble."
According to Lee Gordon, show promoter, Presley is getting a guarantee on the show, "but I can't tell how much. It's in the contract."

On November 5th, Elvis, keeping his promise to his mother not to fly unless it was absolutely necessary, boarded the USS Matsonia in Los Angeles[1] with his entourage for the 4 day boat trip to Hawaii. His mother's, and likely his own, fears were no doubt reaffirmed by the fact that a Pan American flight en route to Hawaii from San Francisco with 44 people aboard had gone down in the ocean the night before his arrival.

During this visit, Elvis fell in love with the beauty of the islands and the hospitality of the people of Hawaii. The Islands are a true paradise for people in search of sun, white sandy beaches, surfing and beautiful scenery. Hawaii would become Elvis' favorite vacation destination and he would enjoy many visits there until his last one in March of 1977. Not only did he make three movies in Hawaii, *Blue Hawaii*, *Girls! Girls! Girls!* and *Paradise, Hawaiian Style*, he also came to Hawaii for two live performances.

The first was on March 25, 1961. The show was a fund raiser to build a memorial for the USS Arizona, the largest of the battleships that had been sunk on December 7, 1941, during the surprise Japanese air attack on Pearl Harbor. The second was also a benefit show beamed world-wide on January 14, 1973. It benefited the Kui Lee Cancer Fund. Kui Lee, who died of this disease in 1966, had composed the song "I'll Remember You."

---

[1] There is still some confusion about the port of departure. A film shown above with Elvis allegedly standing at the railing suggests that the ship left in fact from San Francisco and EPE confirmed it in one of the episodes of *Graceland Gates*.

On the USS Matsonia

Honolulu Star Bulletin, November 4, 1957.

Fortunately for his Hawaiian fans, Elvis, after finishing his tour in late October, had no plans and there were no other appearances scheduled before the January 1959 start of his fourth movie *King Creole*. As a tour promoter Lee Gordon suggested to Col. Parker the idea of the Hawaii trip since it was possible to extend the just-completed tour. Col. Parker told the *Honolulu Star Bulletin* on Thursday, 31 October, that the appearance in Hawaii was developed during a 30 minute lunch break, two days after Elvis' last appearance in the Pan Pacific Stadium in Los Angeles.

In the press conference on the ship Elvis told a week later, the sudden decision to travel like this:
"It was a real rush deal. We were in Hollywood to make a picture, but it was postponed until the first of the year. We weren't doing anything, so Mr. Parker asked if we'd like to go to Hawaii. I said "huh" and was packed right away."

Parker immediately flew to Honolulu to oversee the preparations. But Elvis held on to the promise he gave his mother (and because of his own fear of flying), and made the journey by ship. Hawaii flights with commercial airlines were in 1957 still relatively new, so most people traveled to and from Hawaii with a small fleet of ships that sailed the Pacific route.

On 5 November Elvis went aboard the USS Matsonia and sailed to Honolulu.

Opposite top: Elvis working on his tan on the deck.
Opposite bottom and following pages: Elvis with fellow passengers.

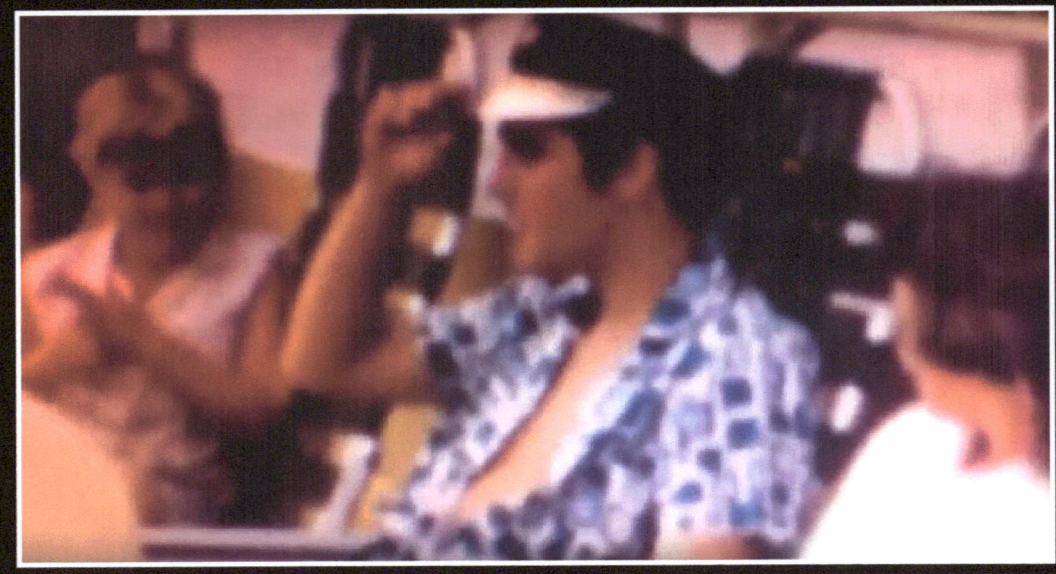

Elvis with Marilyn Waste. The man at the rail on the right is Kenneth Moore. He was at the time Head of Elvis' Security.

Both pictures courtesy of Mrs. Wastes' son, Corby Waste.

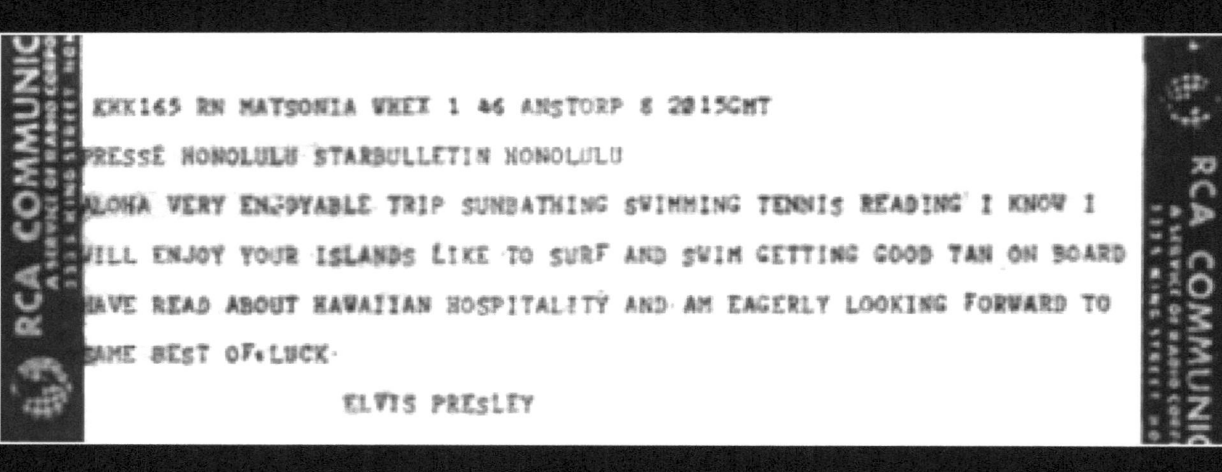

Telegram Elvis sent to the Hawaiian Press from the USS Matsonia the day before his arrival.

The telegram reads:

ALOHA VERY ENJOYABLE TRIP SUNBATHING SWIMMING TENNIS READING I KNOW I WILL ENJOY YOUR ISLANDS LIKE TO SURF AND SWIM GETTING GOOD TAN ON BOARD HAVE READ ABOUT HAWAIIAN HOSPITALITY AND AM EAGERLY LOOKING FORWARD TO COME BEST OF LUCK.

ELVIS PRESLEY.

Bee Bea, the granddaughter of a woman that worked as a waitress on the USS Matsonia in the 1950s recalled her grandmother's comments about Elvis: "He ate with my grandma and the other waitresses in their dining area because he was quite shy about eating in the regular passenger dining room. He signed an autograph for my mom who was a teenager at the time. She still has it!"

In the picture above, Elvis is seen holding a towel like the cape of a bullfighter with his left arm at his back. A passenger played the toro and the two of them went at it for a while on the deck of the ship.

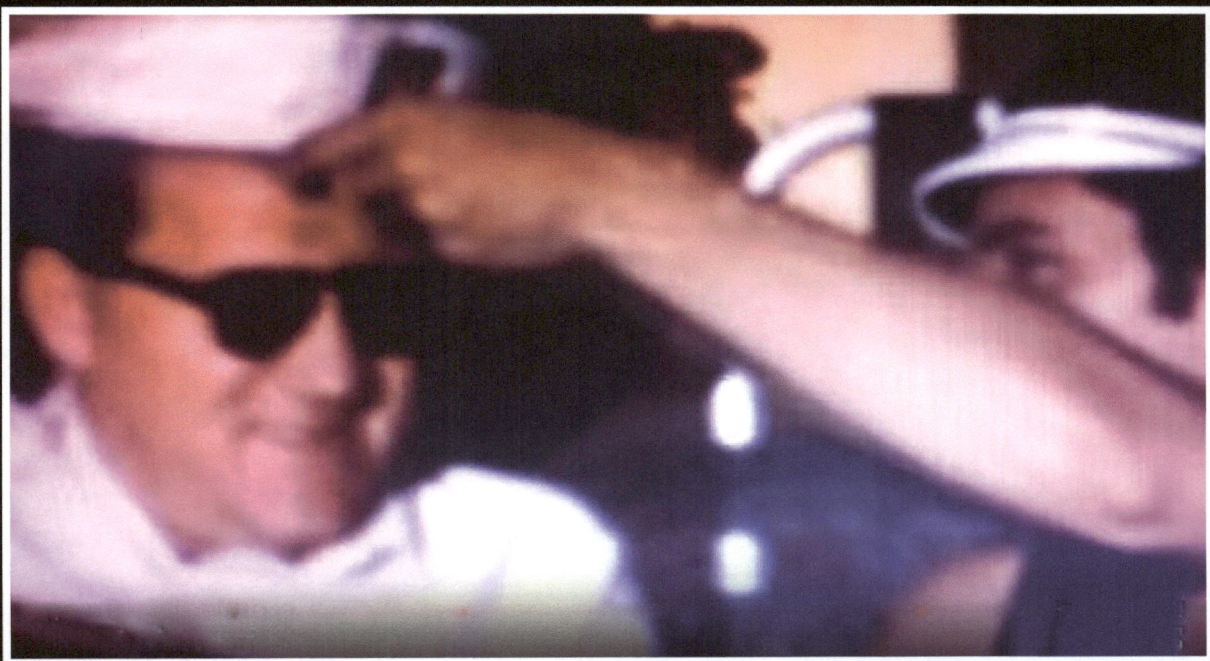

Windy day!

Above: Picture of a man who worked on the USS Matsonia in 1957. He is proudly showing an old photograph of himself with Elvis. Once again, it demonstrates Elvis' innate amiability in posing for the camera with everyone, whether celebrities or members of the general public.
Opposite: The original picture taken in front of the ship's library.

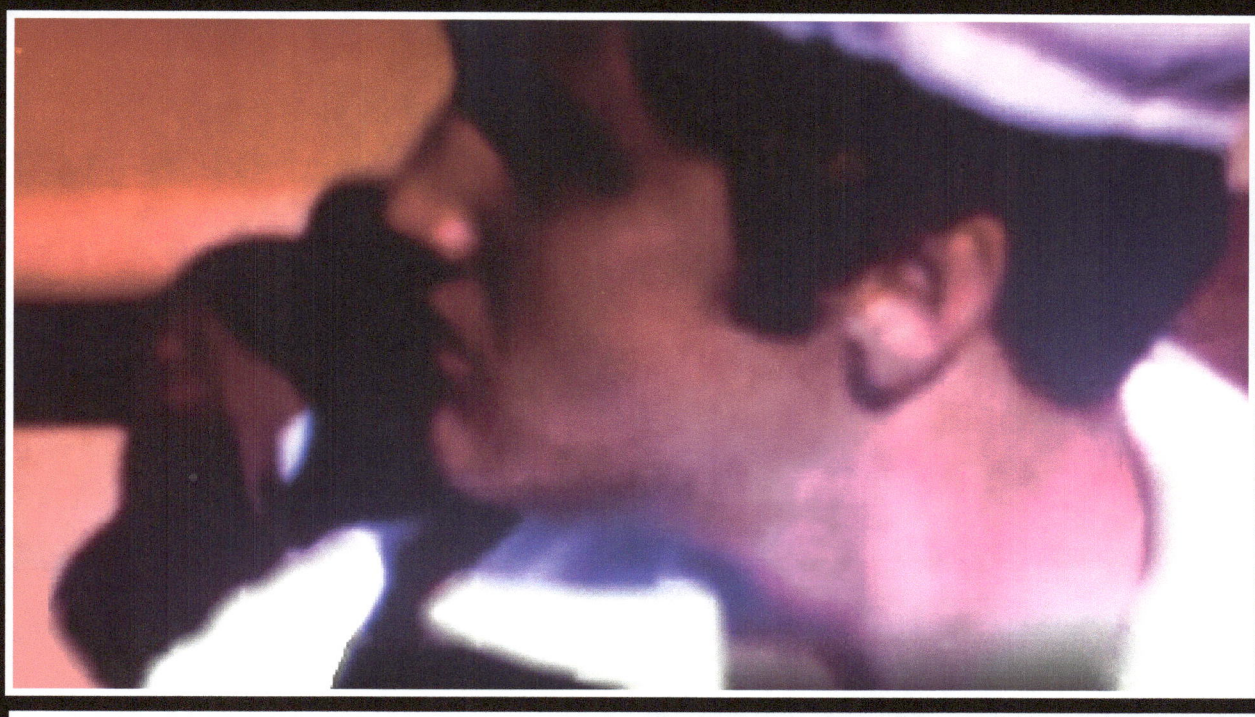

Top: As the USS Matsonia approaches the harbor, Elvis, fully dressed, passes through the ship's kitchen on his way to the deck.

November 9, Arrival

Above: Elvis and a member of a group of Hula dancers who were allowed on the ship to welcome Elvis.
Opposite: Elvis is waving to the fans waiting for him on the docks.

Presley Descends to Comanche Yells Of 4,000 Admirers As Matsonia Docks

Orman Vertrees, *Honolulu Star Bulletin*, November 9, 1957.

"Back . . . back please. Presley is first—then the Congressmen," a harried Matsonia official muttered as he made way for Elvis Presley's debarkation this morning from the Matsonia at Pier 10. The rock 'n roll idol drew in his breath at the top of the gangplank, slicked back his long locks, planted a few moist kisses on nearby hula girls for the cameramen, and descended to the wild shrieks of some 4,000 fans.
Brownie cameras clicked, girls, jostled and pressed forward, the while emitting a variety of Comanche yells. The teenagers weren't outfought but they were slickly outmaneuvered.
Colonel Torn Parker, Presley's manager, murmured a few quick comments to Elvis. Then the manager smoothly guided him to a waiting taxi and they disappeared in a matter of seconds, leaving the crowd milling uncertainly. Presley's fans may not get too close to the guitar-playing Tennessean, but they will see and hear him at two shows tomorrow. at 3 p.m. and 8 pm. in Honolulu Stadium.
Elvis met the press, and two resolute lasses who managed to crash the function, aboard ship an hour before he landed.
He wore a white knit sweater with a large rolled collar, a wine-colored sports coat flocked with black, black slacks, dark well-shined loafers and white socks checkered with brown.

This 22 year-old with the build of an-Oklahoma halfback soon had skeptical newsmen singing his praises. Speaking with a Southern slur and liberally punctuating his answers with "suh," Elvis freely admitted, "I'm pretty green when it comes to clothes. "I don't pay over $7 for a shirt and $10 for a pair of shoes. But I do plan to stock up on a Hawaiian outfit while I'm here." He said present plans call for his party of nine to return to Memphis, Tennessee, next week. Asked if he might visit any Neighbor Islands, he said. "It depends on how we're received here. Presley and Parker both indicated an Australian tour following their visit here is unlikely, although "We're always open to a last minute switch."

He explained their sudden decision to visit the Islands this way: "It was a real rush deal. We were in Hollywood to make a picture (as yet unnamed), but it was postponed until the first of the year. We weren't doing anything, so Mr. Parker asked if

we'd like to go to Hawaii. "I said, 'Huh!' and was packed right away."
As for his traveling companions, mostly high school friends and disc jockeys, Presley said, "I like to have my friends along . . . it gives me a little touch of home. Anyway, it's more fun to see things together. "I've got a waiting list . . . pretty long one . . . of friends who want to make trips with me. "In fact I've heard from lots of so-called old friends from years ago who always say, 'You remember me, don't you?' "
He said his latest hit, "Jailhouse Rock" has sold more than two million records in its first two weeks out. He didn't indicate whether this might be on his Hawaiian program, but he said enthusiastically that "Hawaiian music will certainly be on my program if I can learn any in time."

Other Presley views in a nutshell; Such nicknames as "Elvis the Pelvis" are strictly juvenile.
"There's nothing I can do about it, but it sounds like little kids trying to find something to rhyme with Elvis.
"I have no steady girl friend nor do I have any plans of marriage right now.
"I would eventually like to be a good actor. I haven't had time up to now, but I would like to study for it.
"I don't like airplanes. I'm scared stiff of them. In fact, we could've been on this one missing now.
"I brought only three pieces of luggage. But I guess there must be about 40 for all of us."

There was no confusion and no throngs of juveniles when Presley and his party arrived at the Hawaiian Village Hotel. Several teen-age girls were waiting quietly, and one of them-Babette (Bobby) Andre-presented the singer with a lei and the kiss that goes with it. Presley returned the kiss vigorously. Miss Andre walked away in a happy daze.

The Jordanaires and Presley's guitar, bass and drums accompanists are scheduled to arrive by plane at 4:30 this afternoon[1]

---

1   Scotty, Bill, DJ, and the Jordanaires took a United Airlines flight. Contrary to the usual rule, this time they would stay in the same hotel with Elvis. The entire fourteenth floor of the Hawaiian Village Hotel had bee reserved. Scotty remembered that his room was much nicer than the ones he usually got in the USA.

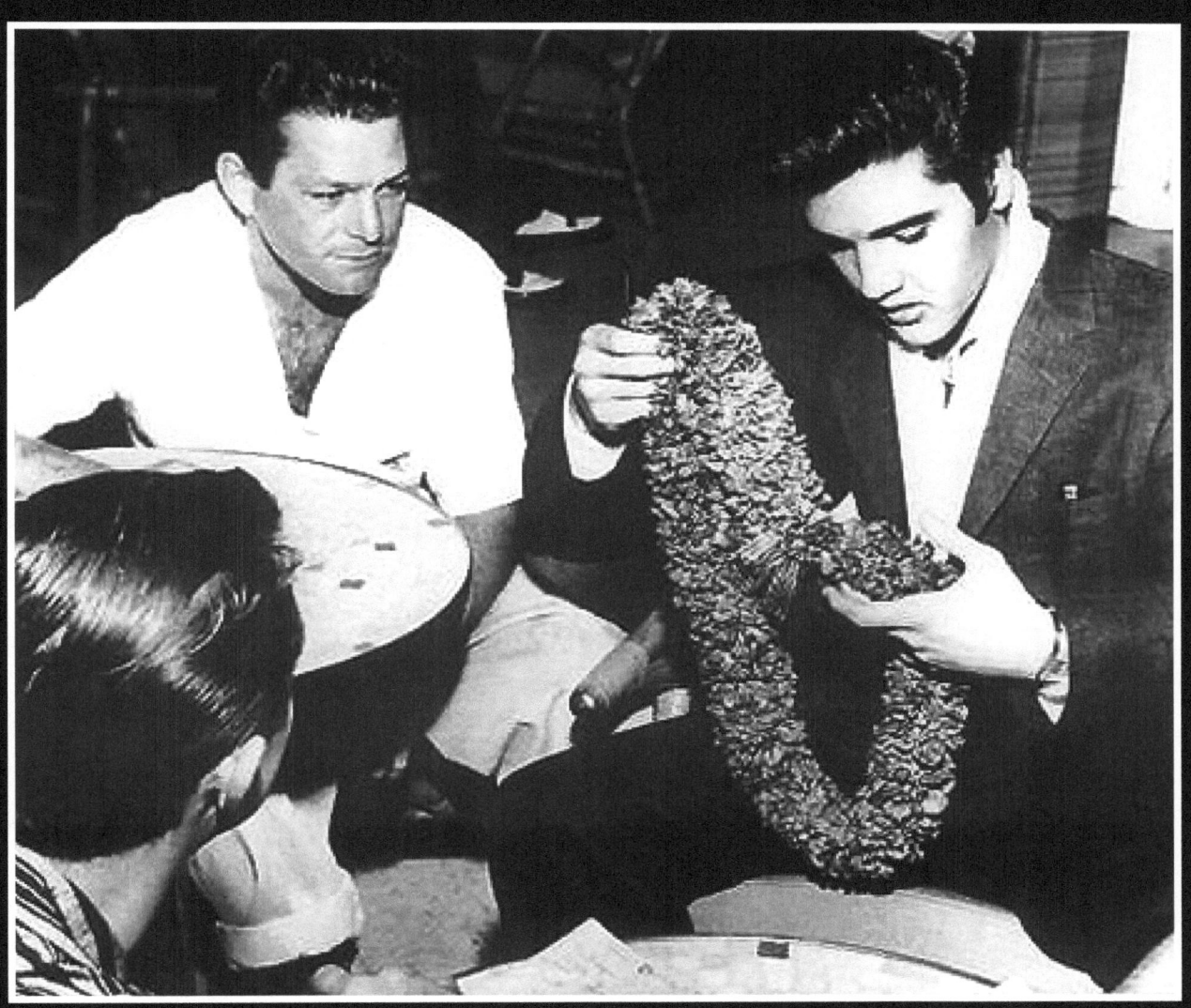
Honolulu Advertiser's Bob Krauss and Eddie Sherman handing leis to Elvis.

Elvis Greeted by Mob Of Screaming Teenagers.

Honolulu Sunday Advertiser - November 11, 1957.

Elvis Presley arrived in Honolulu Saturday morning on the Matsonia. Several thousand orderly but screaming teenagers waited inside Pier 10 for him to disembark. (The first teenage fan took up her vigil at 6:30 a.m. She's a cousin of Alfred Apaka.)
As he hurried off the ship via the crew's gangplank, surrounded by his bodyguards and traveling companions, a scream went up that sounded like a hurricane at its height.
As if they had practiced the maneuver many times before, Presley's party formed a V in front of the singing idol and ran at a trot down the stairs, past the screaming crowd. Then they hopped into a waiting limousine and sped away.
It was much like a well-rehearsed get away for a bank robbery.

Presley's room number at the Hawaiian Village hotel is 14-A, kids, but knowing it won't do you much good.
Barbara Wong of Kaneohe, a teenage Presley fan, made a 63-foot plumeria lei and brought it clear over the Pali only to find that the rock 'n roll star isn't answering his telephone.
With tears in her eyes, she asked the manager of the hotel if he couldn't take her up to see Presley. "Sorry," he said, "there's nothing I can do."

Aboard the USS Matsonia, as the ship entered the harbor, Presley obligingly posed for photographers, preferably with a hula girl in his arms.
"Take your time," he told the photographers at one point, "this in the best part of the trip."
A short time later when Snookie Skoglund, a 15 year old from Minneapolis squeezed beside Presley and gave him a lei and bussed him soundly, he kissed her right back and murmured. "Honey, it's been five days since I've seen a girl. You better watch out."

IN A BRIEF interview with reporters on shipboard, Presley said he took the Matsonia to Hawai rather than an airplane because he's afraid of flying. Asked why, he replied. "Just listen to the headlines. I could have been on that flight (which disappeared Friday afternoon between San Francisco and Honolulu with 44 persons aboard.)
However, he added, he has, no Hawaiian tunes on his program. The only Hawaiian "that I ever sung is 'Until We Meet Again.' That's 'Aloha Oe,' isn't it?"

Elvis was now wearing welcome leis.

A reporter asked, "What do you think of being called Elvis the Pelvis?" Presley answered, "It's very immature and childish. Like a kid trying to find something to rhyme with Elvis."
He explained that the nine persons traveling with him are all friends from Memphis whom he takes with him for company wherever he goes and "to have a little touch of home."
The waiting list of applications for these positions, he added, is quite long.

"What are the prerequisites for the job?" asked one reporter.
"What's that, sir'?" said Elvis blankly.
"The prerequisites for the job?"
"How do you pick 'em?" asked another reporter.
"Oh, they're just old friends . . . from school and around home."
Elvis, who was wearing a maroon jacket, black slacks, black loafers, gray socks and a white knit sweater, said he brought along only three suitcases.

Asked to describe what he had on he said, "Don't ask me. I'm real green about clothes." He said he picks out his own and never pays more than $7 for a shirt, $10 for a pair of shoes.
A fellow passenger, who made the trip with him, described Presley as likeable. "He spent a lot of time posing for movies with the waitresses so they could show their children."

The only note of discord to his welcome to Honolulu appeared in the harbor before the Matsonia tied up. It was a small outboard runabout manned by three teenagers who held aloft a banner reading, "Elvis Go Home."

BACKSTAGE

Eddie Sherman, *Honolulu Advertiser,* November 11, 1957.

The only ones who were "all shook up" when Elvis arrived in Honolulu Saturday were thousands of teenagers who caught a fleeting glimpse of the singer. Presley admitted he loves crowds. "When there's a mob waiting," said Elvis, "it doesn't upset me a bit. Just the people in my group."
Elvis received his first lei in Hawaii from Milwarde Rathburn of Matson. The "ceremony" took place at sea—during his first Hawaiian press conference in the Marine veranda of the Matsonia. "He's a very polite boy," said Milwarde, "and much handsomer than I thought."

The tall husky Elvis punctuated his conversation with many "yes sirs" and "no sirs." He combed his hair a half dozen times, but the long locks had trouble staying in place.
We asked him about that brawl in a Memphis filling station. "'If I have to, I can take care of myself pretty good. As a kid I scrapped about as much as anyone." His 180 pounds seems fairly well distributed over a large six foot frame.

Does Elvis have a favorite entertainer?
"Not really. If the talent is good. I like it."
His ambition?
"I hope to be a good actor, someday."
His pet peeve? Being called Pelvis.

Tom Moffatt and Ron Jacobs were two of the deejays hired by KHVH radio station to cover Elvis' visit. In 1957, Jacobs teamed with Moffatt to jump-start KHVH Radio. The young deejays brought the best young talent to perform concert dates in Honolulu; and developed relationships with the era's best rock talent. It included Elvis Presley and his manager.

Ron recalled that he and Tom pulled a prank that featured "The First Elvis Impersonator." They had the station's engineer dress up like Elvis with a black wig and ride around town in a convertible making frequent stops to phone in his location to the station and then driving away quickly when fans approached.

Elvis' mansger with Tom Moffatt, left, and Ron Jacobs, right in 1959.

However, Tom and Ron's prank created enough of a stir to attract the attention of the Colonel. Fortunately Elvis and his manager liked it. Both deejays emceed concerts at Honolulu Stadium. Ron emceed the matinee show and Tom the evening one. Ron said, "A lifelong friendship began with Parker, who became a mentor." On his many Hawaii trips, Parker arranged exclusive Elvis promotions with Tom and Ron. Both served as honorary pallbearers at Parker's 1997 funeral.

Teen-agers Will See but Not Touch Elvis.

Honolulu Star-Bulletin, November 4, 1957.

Officialdom said today that Elvis Presley's fans will get to see him but not touch him when he arrives on the Matsonia at Pier 10 at 9 am tomorrow. He will come in on the ship, all right, officials said, but their plans are such that they predict no fan will get within 10 feet of him at the pier and few will get within yards of him at the Hawaiian Village Hotel where he will have a 14th floor refuge.

Security plans for Elvis match those for visiting chiefs of state. A web of about 30 men, including personal guards, police officers and Castle & Cooke security officers will surround the dock area. Assistant Chief of Police Dewey Mookini said 22 additional men will be on call should there be any mob action. Castle & Cooke is also ready with an extra guard crew - just in case things get out of hand.
Terminal officials reported a double fence may also be put up as an additional safeguard.
They said security measures mapped for the Presley entrance will make it impossible for fans to get closer than 10 feet from the rock 'n' roll idol.

Chief Mookini believes that this reinforced security was never accorded any other person arriving here. Even (ex-President) Truman had about 20 men," he recalled.
But dockside preparations appear niggardly compared to the security strategy outlined at the Hawaiian Village Hotel, where the singer will be quartered in a 14th floor penthouse. About a dozen men, including Al Pinoli, chief of security at the hotel, will be on 24—hour duty, guarding each entrance, staircase and elevator. Two side entrances to the hotel will be barricaded, thereby, cutting the stream of traffic through the main entrance only. In the 14th floor Presley hideout, three of his personal guards who are traveling with him will on watch.

As Mr. Pinoli puts it: "Teenagers may as well forget about seeing him up close. They aren't going to have a chance. This place is teen-aged proof."
He said all teenagers wandering around by themselves will be suspect and that only guests will be allowed to go up to the floors.
If a guest wants friends up to his room, he will have to come-down to meet them and personally escort them up.

He noted "this is going to be rough on the rest of the guests too, but we can't take any risk of property or personal damage."

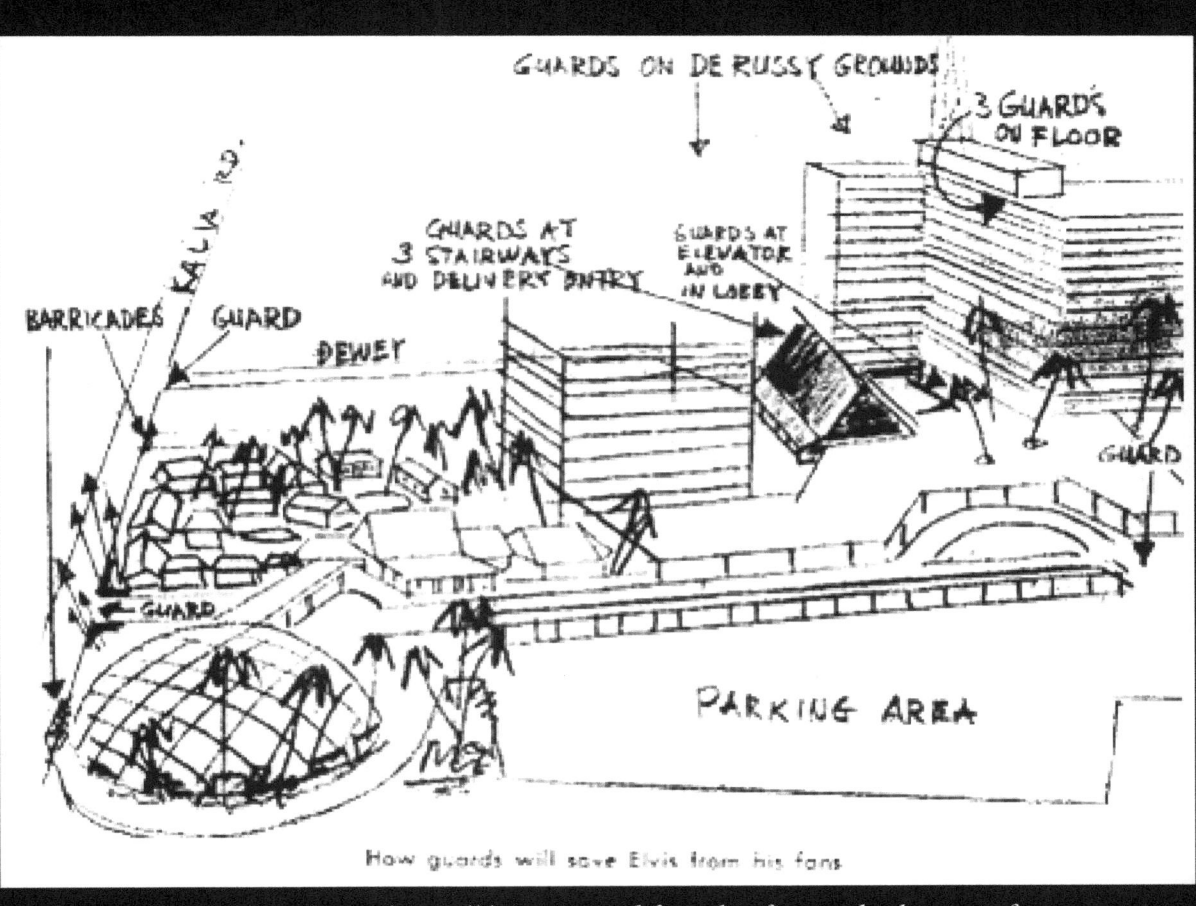

Drawing showing how Elvis will be protected from his fans and other interferences.

Elvis and a vahine doing the Hula.

Elvis had a press conference aboard the USS Matsonia after its arrival in Honolulu harbor at 8.45 a.m. After the press conference Elvis and his party headed to the Hawaiian Village Hotel where Elvis checked in on the fourteenth floor.

As soon as he settled into room 1406 at the Hawaiian Village, Elvis gave a telephone call to his mother to assure her that everything was alright.
This picture was taken by Kaneohe Fan Club President Barbara Wong.

The 17 year-old student Barbara Wong of the B. Castle High School was in the fall of 1957 not only the biggest Elvis fan of the Hawaiian Islands, but also the President of Kaneohe Elvis Presley fan clubs on Oahu. Although only one was answered, she had written a weekly letter to Elvis for two years. On November 4, 1957 it became known that Elvis would appear on the following Sunday in Honolulu Stadium. As a result, Barbara had a lot of planning to do. Elvis would arrive in 5 days and stay for 4 days in Honolulu. She knew that she would see Elvis not just once, but that she would see him every day. And not just see -she would touch him, give him gifts, talk to him, and yes - even kiss him.

Barbara had not worked out the details, but she knew for certain that, throughout his stay in the city, Elvis was the highest priority in her life.

Opposite: Al Dvorin, Tom Parker, Lee Gordon and Tom Diskin in Hawaii in November 1957.

He's a Promoter and a Gentleman.

Cobey Black, *Honolulu Star Bulletin* November 11, 1957.

As Mike Todd whirled out of the Hawaiian Village, in ambled a soft-spoken, molasses · moving Southern gentleman who knew all the tricks of show business before Mike could spell his own name. (He still can't. That's why it's Todd.) Colonel Tom Parker deserves his honorary Tennessee title. He's won countless victories on the precarious field of entertainment, the latest and greatest being the triumph of Elvis Presley.

Half a dozen years ago the good colonel was booking teen-age Elvis in a package deal on a small-town circuit. Last year his protégé received 400,000 Christmas cards — 20,000 of them from Hawaii.

"This year the Youth Foundation chose as the world's four top personalities: Elvis, President Eisenhower, Queen Elisabeth and Princess Grace," said Colonel Parker. . He was modestly stating a fact.

And the longer I lingered over lunch with Colonel Parker and Tom Diskin, a gentle, sandy-haired young man who is tour manager for the Presley show, the more I enjoyed their homespun candor. After a week on Todd's pressure cooker. it was a relief to be among the grits and gravy folk. Naturally, the conversation turned to— who else? "Call it personality - magnetism. Valentino had it. Only the kids can tell you what it is. It hasn't spoiled Elvis. I can tell you that. Just made him more mature, more seriously interested in his career. Did you know that of his 20 personal appearances this year, eight of them benefited charities, and four of them gave all the proceeds to charity?"

THE COLONEL WAS interrupted by Tom Diskin, who added "I've read at least 50 letters to Elvis from blind and handicapped children who are confined to their beds or homes, and they all used the same phrase 'You've made life worth living.' Elvis is a very sensitive boy who thinks about these things. In two years we've sent out 50,000 books and pictures to organizations, and we've paid for the shipping and merchandise."

"Yet when he sang 'Peace In the Valley' on the Ed Sullivan show," continued the Colonel, "he received 5,000 letters from religious groups asking him to build churches.

"One lady has been writing constantly asking Elvis to sell five of his six cars because her father is along in years and could use the money. I wonder if she knows that last month he raised $20,000 in Tupelo for a youth center.

"He's such a pro-and-con personality that all kinds of stories crop up. I read in your papers that I'd been talking to Hal Lewis over dinner about Elvis. I've never had dinner with Hal Lewis. I called him right away to ask who'd picked up the tab.

"Several months ago an article in a Georgia paper described Elvis's life in the Army, and said I was working in the commissary selling pictures. We were on tour 2.000 miles away. Elvis is 1-A of course, but he's still on the waiting list.

"Yesterday I had over 30 calls, mostly from kids, asking if Elvis was REALLY coming—if it wasn't just a joke.

"He's really coming, on the Matsonia, with a party of 10 friends and relations. Boy, will they be all shook up when they land. He won't fly, you know. We once chartered a plane in Texas and two motors went out. We ditched in a field."

And that cured him? I asked.

"Cured him, honey? It scared the living daylights out of him. The only thing he was sure of was his safety belt and it was so tight it nearly cut him in two."

Do you know if he has any plans for marriage? I asked Tom D.

"When he meets someone and falls in love. everybody'll know. He wont hide it. He thinks love is something to be proud of."

And will you, Colonel Parker, continue to be his manager as long as his career lasts?

"My career will go on with or without Elvis, and his will with or without me. He's going on 22 and I'm going on 50, so he'll be going on a lot longer than I. Also I'm all shook up already."

"For my next promotion, I'm going to try to get that little dog in Sputnik II. Seriously, honey, he'd be great on a personal appearance tour. And I could get a good deal on dog food."

November 10, The Concerts

Program for Sunday's Elvis Presley Show.

Honolulu Star Bulletin - November 11, 1957.

The Elvis Presley show in Honolulu Stadium is divided into two parts, with a 15 minute intermission.

Elvis will appear in the second portion of the show and will sing for at least half an hour, a spokesman says.

The program:

Opening medley by Ray Tanaka and his 11-piece Honolulu show orchestra. Introduction by comedian Howard Hardin, of Chicago, who will be master of ceremonies and also do specialty numbers.

Island entertainers to be seen in the first half of the show include Sterling Mossman, known as "the hula cop"; Kaui Barrett, dancer; Phyllis Brooks, singer; Eddie Spencer's Queen's Men, all from the Queen's Surf floor show.
Then the Jordanaires, Capitol recording artists, who are touring with Presley, will sing.

Intermission follows:

After the intermission, Ray Tanaka's group will play before Hardin introduces Elvis. Elvis's selections will vary according to audience reaction. He will sing several of his RCA Victor record hits.

Accompanying Presley are the Blue Moon Boys, musicians who have been with him since the beginning.

Both shows follow the same general format.

Running time of each show: from 90 to 120 minutes.

Opposite: Concert poster published in the *Honolulu Sunday Advertiser*, November 3, 1957.
Next two pages: Advertisements in the newspapers.

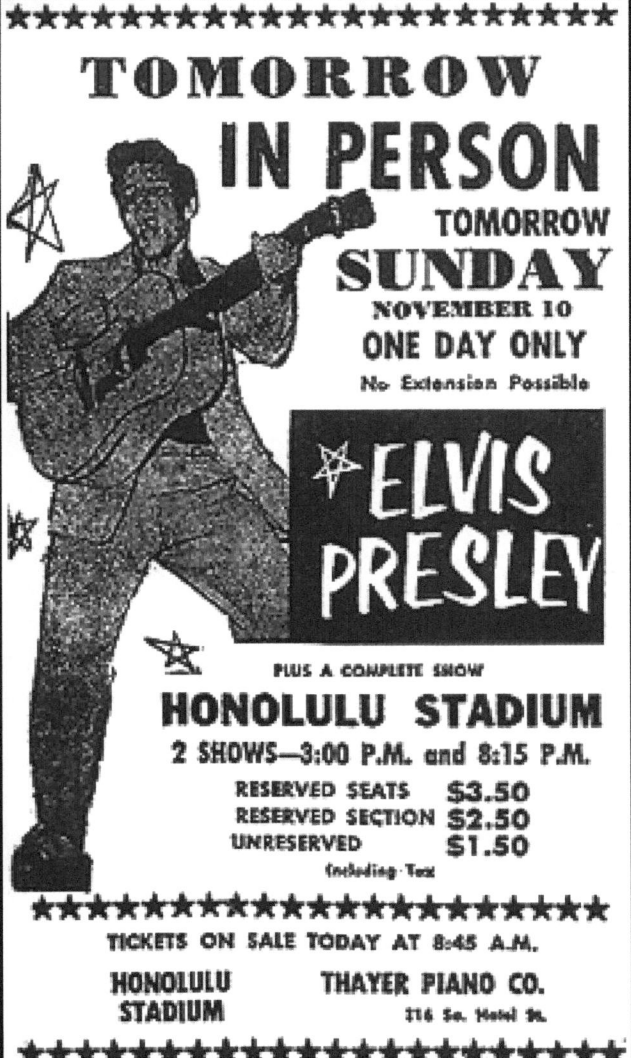

Elvis gave two concerts on November 11, the first one at 3:00 P.M., the second one at 8:15 P.M. Most of the pictures do not specify which concert they were taken from, so they are therefore lumped together.

Elvis arrived at the Honolulu Stadium in a car and walked to the stage where his musicians were waiting for him.

Presley Proves He's 'King' To Squealing Teen-Agers.

Walt Christie, *Honolulu Star-Bulletin*, November 11, 1957.

Those frenetic fans who "loved" Elvis Presley before seeing him in person yesterday are even more ardent today. And those who weren't "sent" before still aren't. About 15,000 Honolulans spent $32,000 yesterday to see for themselves just what sort of entertainer sparks the Presley cult. Response, it must be chronicled, was mixed. On the plus side of the ledger is the fact that the hula-hipped, crazy-legged Elvis is a versatile singer.

Right now—obviously—that doesn't matter. If there ever were a "pre-sold" attraction, Elvis is it. He could do no wrong as far as last night's shrieking, beat-clapping enthusiasts were concerned.

He scratched his ear—and squeals of joy echoed through the uninhibited audience that jam-packed the makai side of Honolulu Stadium. He shrugged a shoulder of his sparkling metallic-threaded jacket—and the girls literally bounced up and down in their seats. The king can do no wrong. And Elvis, make no mistake, IS the king of

He's America's top money entertainer and, more significantly, tradesters predict he'll be around for several years to come. Once his fanatical following abates, Presley can emerge as a mighty competent "straight" singer. On the negative side is the fact that Americas two-legged answer to the Sputnik violates every rule in the book when it comes to showmanship.

the teen-agers who—the same teenagers who snap up each of his recordings by the millions and who sacrifice lunch money so they can buy a ticket to see him. Elvis, it appears, enjoys this mass hero worship. Indeed there are times when you wonder how he can keep a straight face as he watches his audience.

Presley had 'em rockin' if not always rollin' to the tempos of many of his best-known songs. Matter of fact, he was on stage for about 40 minutes, accompanied by his own trio and the Jordanaires quartet. Surprisingly, he spent more time at the piano than he did with his guitar. His routine is paced effectively, gradually mounting in tempo to a climax that sees him jumping off-stage and toward the front rows of the audience, then making a hasty retreat to a waiting auto.

The audience's mass emotion wasn't dampened in the least by two flurries of rain, a whirl of dust, the poor lighting of the on-field stage, and mediocre public-address facilities. It would be a mistake to generalize about audience reaction.

The king is all things to all people. It's not only teenagers who were "oohing" and bouncing and shrieking to his beat and loose-legged gyrations.

Many of the teenagers' mothers were, too. And a 7 or 8 year-old girl sitting near this writer was equally responsive. The male audience, for the most part, was far more reserved or, at least, stoic. In some cases, it was bored. That, in the long run, may be Presley's biggest handicap. Right now, without going into social significance or sex appeal or personal magnetism, he's strictly for the girls. If you're still wondering about his bewildering effects upon the bewildered parents and their bewildering offspring, you can see him in action tonight at Schofield Barracks. Of one thing you can be sure. It'll be the most memorable thing that's happened at Schofield since December 7, 1941.

90

Hipster Hexes Hysterical Hepsters.

Bob Krauss, *Honolulu Advertiser*, November 11, 1957.

Elvis Presley left Honolulu teenagers all shook up yesterday after two rock 'n roll concerts at Honolulu stadium. Thousands of kids nearly went out of their minds screaming at the loose-jointed antics of their singing idol as he wiggled and wobbled and clowned his way through an hour-long performance.

His two performances drew 14,963 spectators, evenly divided, between the two shows, who paid $32,000. Elvis is reported to get more than half of it.

Primed by an opening half program of juggling, hula sword dancing and jive, the teenage audience (mostly girls) set up a shrill, continuous scream as Elvis romped on the open air stage dressed in a gold lame jacket trimmed in silver, a black shirt, black slacks and black loafers. He stood still for a moment, then threw an experimental wobble at his fans. As if he had pushed a button, the audience erupted with screams. From then on the concert resembled some kind of primitive religious ceremony with the audience gradually working itself into a greater and greater frenzy.

Oddly enough, there was very little clapping after each number. But Presley had only to say, "thank you very much," and the audience would scream. He'd scratch his nose; another scream. He'd laugh; another scream. At times, the singer seemed to deliberately push the button by dropping his arm or wiggling his shoulder, just to hear his fans react. Then he'd laugh, it seemed to me, partly at himself and partly at the audience.

For all of his inept clowning on the stage, the singer is obviously an expert at teasing the greatest possible hysteria from his teenage worshippers. The best example was his closing number. "You Ain't Nothin' But a Hound Dog," which brought the audience to its feet from the opening note. Presley threw his hips around, wobbled his knees, flopped his shoulders and shook all over until the girls in the stands were hopping up and down with excitement. Then, for the first time, he sat down on the edge of the stage. Teenagers began pressing forward to see better and the police (I counted 30 inside the stadium) nervously closed ranks. Finally, he hopped dawn upon the grass in front of the stage. The crowd nearly went crazy. Girls climbed up to stand on the sides of the box I was sitting in. Others were standing precariously on chairs. Meanwhile. Presley was rolling on the grass moaning out the words of "Hound Dog." He kissed a girl across the barricade set up to keep the audience away from the stage, grabbed a coconut hat and paraded with it on his head.

Wave after wave of screams rolled across the stadium as he finished the song. Then, he turned, stepped into a waiting car and sped out of sight before most of the excited teenagers knew he was gone. Often criticized for lewdness in connection with his hip swinging gyrations, Presley, in my opinion, was not objectionable at the stadium. He was loose but he wasn't lewd. Tonight, Presley will give a final show at Schofield Barracks.

An Hawaiian fan recalls.

I was lucky enough to go to the Elvis concert in 1957 at our old Honolulu Stadium. It was in pre-Statehood Hawaii, called the Territory of Hawaii. The stadium site at King & Isenberg streets is now a park, as it was torn down in the mid-70s when the Aloha Stadium in Halawa opened.

The old termite palace had been around since 1926, and had seen a lot of things. For the Elvis show, they built a stage for him on a big tractor trailer flatbed. The stage was at the 50 yard line, near the running track around the field, facing the press box side of the football field, so the audience could only occupy the sideline bleachers on that side of the field. I don't remember anyone in the end zones bleachers, or on the other side of the field. I do remember a lot of teenage girls screaming. (His back was to the mountains, and he was facing in the direction of the ocean.) He did 2 shows, but I was in elementary school, so I could only go to the matinee in the afternoon. I couldn't go to the evening show. My strongest memory is when Elvis sat down on the edge of the stage, and the crowd hushed, as he whispered a story, and the drama grew... He said something to the effect that, "This next song is a real sad love song that my dear mama used to sing to me... (long pause).
"Then the stage erupted with "You ain't nuthin' but a Hound Dog, crying all the time..." That was the most amazingly dramatic and exciting moment in my life up to that point, as I was only 9 years old, but already a huge fan. (My father worked in radio in Hawaii.)

Elvis visited us several more times during his life, and loved our music.

Mahalo, Harry B.

The Press Conference

In between Sunday's performances at the stadium, Elvis returned to the Hawaiian Village Hotel for a press conference.

Elvis Is 'The Most" Says New Presley Fan.

Lynn Clausen, *Honolulu Star-Bulletin,* November 12, 1957.

Teenagers say Elvis is the most, to say the least. But would the singing sensation of the rock and roll crowd "send" a girl his own age?

"Heavens, no," thought I, and I sallied forth to meet Mr. Presley with tongue in cheek and a closed mind.

I went, I saw—and I was impressed. Elvis is really charming. To begin with, he's good looking, much more so than his pictures-tall, broad-shouldered, and slim-hipped, with deep-set dark blue eyes fringed with long lashes.

His clothes weren't loud, as I had rather uncharitably expected; for an informal press reception at the Hawaiian Village he chose a gray sport jacket and light beige slacks, a black, open necked shirt, and well polished black loafers, with black socks.

Loud colors he loves for cars, but "I like dark clothes, honey."

He has a slow, almost hesitant smile, which matches his way of speaking. And he has a rather appealing trick of giving you a side-long, questioning glance before he answers you.

At all times, he's tactful, hurting no one and stepping on no one's toes. He thinks the Islands are wonderful, Hawaii's girls beautiful, the Hawaiian people "so friendly," and his Hawaiian fans "so well behaved and kind."

I asked the handsome young eligible what he was looking for in a wife—"A female, honey." No, he has nothing special or specific in mind, he'll "just know when his love comes along."

When I asked for his autograph, he obliged quickly and graciously, even inscribing my name at the top. And before I could thank him, he thanked me for asking.

He's really just a very nice boy, this soft-spoken, good looking idol of the younger set. In fact, minus pompadour and side burns, he's something even a young lady his own age wouldn't mind "taking home to mother."

Top: Kaneohe Fan Club President Barbara Wong gave a warm greeting to Elvis.
Opposite: Barbara Wong did not want to let go of Elvis. A more reserved fan is on the right.
Next pages: Other pictures of Elvis with Barbara Wong.

Elvis was 15 minutes late for his press conference at the Hawaiian Village, which gave me time to chat with a young lady who had arrived an hour early to assure herself of a front row seat. "I'm Barbara Wong, president of the Kaneohe Elvis Presley Fan Club," said the pony-tailed teen-ager, adjusting a 63 foot lei and a pair of binoculars. She was wearing a pink dress appliquéd with profiles of Elvis in black. "Pink and black, his favorite colors" she sighed. "I made it myself when 'Love Me Tender' came out. I've written him a letter every week for two years. He answered one. I haven't had a wink of sleep for four days." She turned a pair of glazed eyes on me in proof of her sleepless devotion.

Just what do you see in Elvis? I asked.
"Ohhhh," she moaned. "His dreamy looks. His voice. His southern accent. He's just a livin' MAN?"

With that, the livin' man strode into the room and the president of the Kaneohe Elvis Presley Fan Club threw herself on him like a meringue pie. The members of the press shifted uneasily as Elvis, powerless as Laocoon in the coils of Miss Wong and her 63-foot lei, attempted to extricate himself. Finally he lifted her bodily and carried her to her front row seat.

"Any questions?", he asked. He's strapping boy with the soft profile of a melted Greek coin. He sat on the edge of a desk and swung his legs restlessly. "Yes, Elvis," gasped Miss Wong, oblivious to the rest of us. "Did you get my letters, and the teddy bear?"

"I GOT THE TEDDY bear," said Elvis gently. "I want to say my reception in Hawaii was one of the most well-behaved of my career," he continued for all to hear. "I've been on stage long enough to tell if an audience has manners, and today I could have safely leapt off the stage into the midst of them."

"If only you had, Elvis," whispered Miss Wong.

"What are your vital statistics?" called a voice.

"Six feet tall, I reckon, and 180 pounds."

"Do you exercise when you're not singing?"

"No. That's enough."

"What are your favorite colors?"

"Depends on what it is. Cars I like in loud colors, clothes in dark colors."

"How often do you have a haircut?"

"Not often, and when I do, it doesn't look like a haircut."

"What's the first thing you'll look for in a wife?"

"Female."

"How about her southern cooking?"

"I don't like fried chicken. I like pineapples and coconut."

"What's your ancestry?"

"Irish, I reckon. And some Eyetalian. Never gave it a thought."

"Has success affected your life?"

"Of course. I never realized anything like this was possible, that I'd ever be in Hawaii—or Las Vegas, or Hollywood. It`s quite a change to jump into this stuff. If you're not careful, you'll crack up."

"Is it true you're asking $100,000 for a TV appearance?"

"I'll have to ask my manager," said Elvis, turning to his manager. His manager nodded. "Colonel Parker brought out the fact that why be on TV and let 60 million people see me free when we charge the movie makers so they can charge the audience to see me. Understand? I don't."

"Did you invent rock 'n roll'?"

"I explored it. It existed long before I did. It was called rhythm and blues. I just tried a new interpretation."

"Do you feel an obligation to your public?"

"I do feel an obligation. I'm very careful not to do anything that would disappoint my fans. I behave myself. People have preconceived ideas about me. It's natural. I've often said "I won't like that person," and then found out he's a nice guy."

"What's your reaction to those older people who don't like you?" This was from Miss Wong again.

"Honey, I can't please everybody. Maybe they're Pat Boone fans."

At this point Kini Popo presented Elvis with a scroll from fans on the neighbor Islands. The list of signatures was six feet long.

"With whom would you like most to be cast ashore on an island?" piped up a voice from the rear.

"Any one of these girls around here would do," said Elvis. "Any more questions?"

"One more," pleaded Miss Wong. "What is your reaction to this paragraph from a fan magazine: Elvis takes his date home and drives to a secluded spot,"— there was a tremor in Miss Wong's voice- "Where he gives her the love-me-tender kind of kiss a girl won't fight . . ."

"That's enough" broke in Elvis' manager. "Will the radio people now come forward to record their questions."

Uudaunted, Miss Wong pressed forward with the radio people. She was unfastening a chain around her throat. "I've been wearing this necklace all week," she confided, winding her arms- around Elvis's neck as she fumbled with the clasp behind his head. "I want you to have it, Elvis. It's my lucky ivory fang."

From "Love Him Tender Like a Tiger" Who's News with Cobey Black, *Honolulu Star-Bulletin*, November 11, 1957.

Following the press conference, Elvis penned a short note to Antoinette Mendonca, age nine. She had been a patient at the Mahluhia Hospital since an operation the previous August to relieve pressure from a brain tumor. For the first time in months, Antoinette grinned and she tried to talk after seeing the note that read, in part, "Please get well, honey. I'll be thinking of you."

Excerpt from "Did Elvis Sing in Your Hometown?" by Lee Cotten, High Sierra Books,1995.

Top: Elvis interviewed by Tom Moffatt.

Elvis, Gene Smith and comedian Howard Hardin who was the master of ceremonies and also a performer in the shows.

Note from the hand of Barbara Wong on an Elvis picture from the press conference. It reads:

That's my 63 foot plumeria lei wrapped around Elvis.
Remember that Hawaiian tradition? We always give a lei and a kiss to someone we like! Some of that lipstick is mine!

Barbara

The Fans

November 11, The Concert

The concert was given at the military base named Schofield Barracks after John M. Schofield, a Major General who fought on the Federal side during the Civil War. James Jones, the author of *From Here To Eternity* was stationed for two years at Schofield with the 27th Infantry. His observations of Army life and the December 7, 1941 attack were later the basis for the afore mentioned book. The 1953 movie version starring Montgomery Clift, Deborah Kerr, Frank Sinatra and Burt Lancaster was filmed at
the U.S. Army's Schofield Barracks.

The concert was attended by about 10,000 spectators made up of military personnel and their families and civilians.

Elvis Rocks The Bowl
Rock 'n Roll Artist Has Fans Squealing

Hawaii-Lightning News, November 14, 1957.

You gotta give it to him-he's a great showman! Elvis Presley, the one man hurricane who took the rhythm and blues and turned it into a multi—million rock 'n roll rampage literally wiggled his way into the Post Bowl Monday night and shook up the some 10,000 squealing, screaming fans. The hottest thing to hit this post since the Honest John, Elvis led his audience, majority teen-age girls, into a state of mass hysteria. The loose-jointed idol, dressed in a pearl gray suit and black shirt with his guitar in hand, shimmied and clowned his way through his top hit tunes. His rendition of "Jailhouse Rock" brought the house down. He threw his hips, wobbled his knees, flopped his shoulders then shook and rolled. The more he rolled-the more the audience screamed. Other songs Elvis sang were "Hound Dog," "Don't Be Cruel," "Teddy Bear," "Heartbreak Hotel" and "Love Me."
Also appearing on the two-hour show were the Lucky Charms, one of Schofield's top vocal groups, the popular Lightningaires Band and the Sterling Mossman show from Waikiki's Queen Surf. Monday night's show was a kick-off for Special Services campaign to bring top-notch entertainers to Schofield. Expected to appear at the Bowl in the near future are Nat Cole, Fats Domino and Sammy Davis Jr.

November 12, A Day Off

Above: Elvis and fans. In 2007, Rob Rohm from robrohm.com went to the Elvis Presley statue dedication at the *Neal Blaisdell Center* in Honolulu on July 26th. The statue is to commemorate the Elvis concert that was held at the arena in 1973. About this event, he reported, "I met a lady named Fumie Nakao and she gave me a photo of her with Elvis." The photo was taken on the 14th floor of the Hilton Hawaiian Village in November, 1957 at 11:30 PM. In the photo above, she is on the far right. In the chapter Elvis Statue near the end of the book, there is a picture of Fumis Nakao holding the same photograph .

Next page: Elvis spent some time with a young Hawaiian girl affected by polio.

Elvis did not sailed back to the mainland until Wednesday, so he had a free day on Tuesday. Meanwhile it was obvious, that for him - as always - it was not possible to go surfing or swimming at the beach, a wish that he mentioned in his telegram from the Matsonia.

In spite of the security, not all fans were dissuaded from going to Elvis' hotel. Groups of teenagers buzzed around day and night everywhere on the hotel grounds, forcing Elvis to take his meals in his hotel room. Of course, he couldn't expect that they would leave him in peace, so that he could spend some time alone on the beach - like a regular tourist. One afternoon, he responded in his own way to cries of "We want Elvis", coming from fans on the beach below his room. Elvis went out on his balcony and threw souvenirs to the girls.

Opposite, Elvis' fans, who hounded him at the Hawaiian Village Hotel show the booty Elvis threw down from his room. Among the things were records, album covers, two ties, a beach towel and a handkerchief. As there weren't enough items to go around, the girls broke the records into pieces, ripped the album covers, cut the ties to pieces and the tissue into small pieces so that they all had a souvenir of Elvis.
Kneeling, from left, Sandra Farias with a record; Pat Blake, a record and part of a tie; Judy Blake also with part of tie. Standing, from left, Linda Snyder with a piece of record cover; Raynette Raynor with a piece from a gold tie; Viola Kalama with a part of a record; Bernadette Santos with a handkerchief; Anna McMullin with part of a record; and Francine Carvalho with a piece from a gold tie.

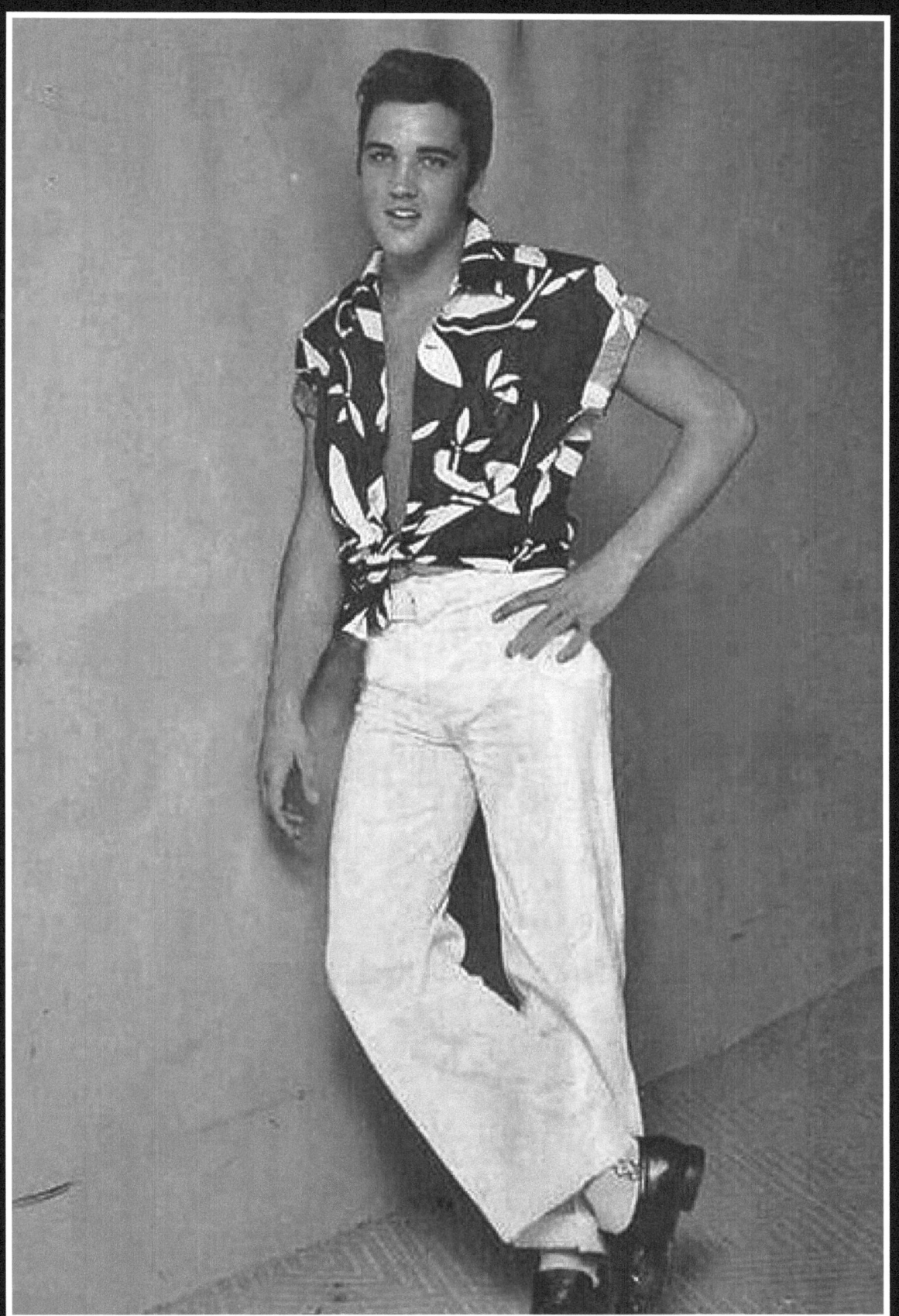

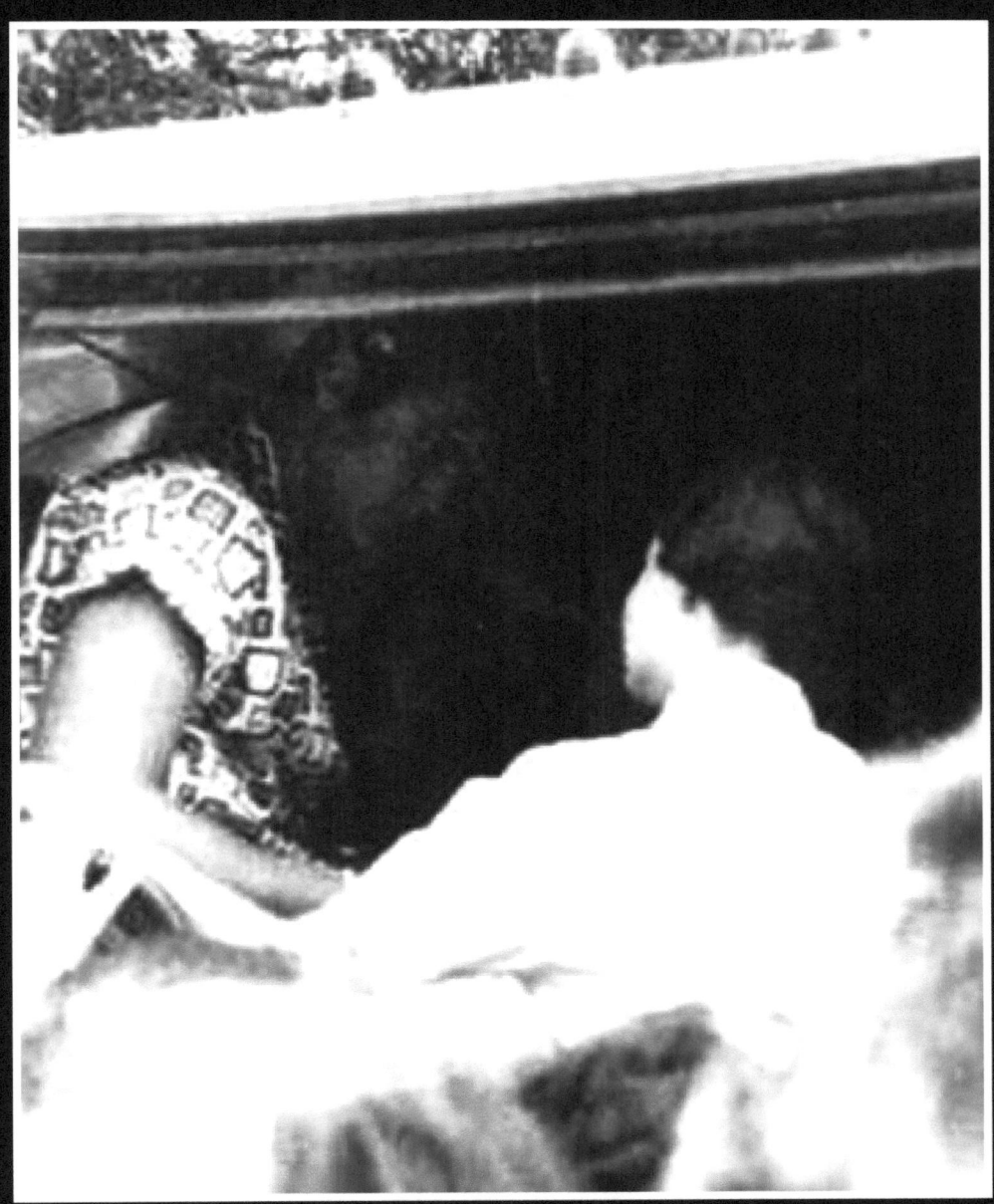

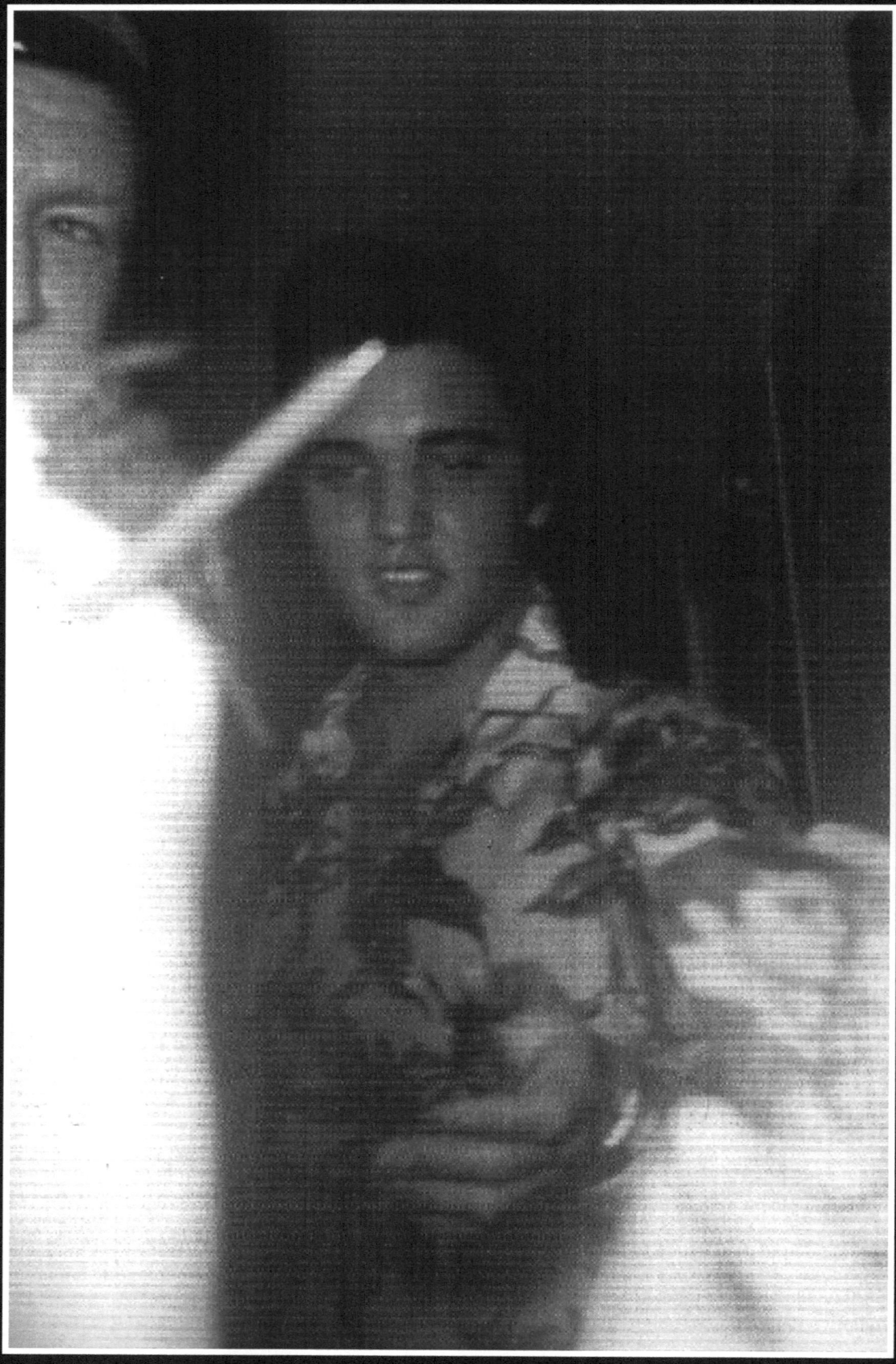

November 13, Departure

On the deck of the USS Lurline. Elvis is wearing the ivory fang necklace that Barbare Wong gave him at the press conference on November 9.

Presley Leaves Today on Lurline, School Helps Keep Teen-Agers Away.

Honolulu Star Bulletin, November 13, 1957.

Unlike his security-studded entrance four days ago, Elvis Presley was to make his 4 p.m. exit on the Lurline today with only a minimum battery of security men. The force will include his three personal guards, compared to the web of 30 men who surrounded him upon his arrival Saturday. Assistant Police Chief Dewey Mookini said only a normal crew of police officers will detail the liner's departure. "We haven't had any requests for extras," he said. Presley, whose bowl-full-of-jelly hip rhythm will be limited to the Lurline's rock 'n roll motions for the next four-and-a-half days,

Elvis waving to fans from the USS Lurline: From left to right, Lamar Fike, Mrs. Moore, Tom Diskin, Elvis, Ken Moore, unidentified and Arthur Hooten.

is bound for a long stay in his hometown, Memphis, Tennessee. Presley's managers explained that the paring down of security is partly due to their faith in Hawaiian hospitality and largely due to their faith in the school system, which will keep teen-agers in classes until 3 p.m. However, at least one teen-ager is making sure she'll be there. Barbara Wong, reported by Castle High School as a "good student" and who has thrown 60-foot leis around Presley personally three times, is not in school today so she could make another garland.

Hawaiian Village Hotel guards reported about 200 teen-agers again up to midnight last night attempted to slip through the security net to get to the 14th floor Presley hide-out. None was successful. Obliging Presley, however, couldn't resist the wails of

10 teenagers, nine girls and a boy, at 11:30 last night and walked down to the beach in shorts to chat and sign autographs. Guards report "all went smoothly."

As it turned out, there were an estimated 5,000 fans at Elvis' departure. That was 1000 more than when he arrived four days earlier. The entire pier was filled from top to bottom, and the whole crowd sang "We want Elvis" and "Elvis, Elvis, Elvis yeah".
The *Star Bulletin* reported that the singer signed autographs, kissed trembling lips, as a steady stream of fans showered him with Leis. Many of the fans were allowed to go on board until about 30 minutes before departure. Flanked by two of his bodyguards, Elvis greeted the fans in the cabin corridor outside his cabin. After the visitors went off board, loyal fans were still standing on the pier to catch a last glimpse of their idol. As the ship took off at the pier, the band played "To Your Sweetheart Aloha" and Elvis appeared near the captain's bridge on the railing.
Dressed in a colorful Hawaiian shirt, he threw kisses and flowers to the slowly receding crowd of people on the pier. Barbara Wong was also among the fans that Elvis, who was leaning against the railing, said good-bye. For the 17-year-old fan club president, it was the culmination of four magical days. She had seen her idol every day - in his hotel room, on the stage, on the press conference, at the beach and on board of the ship. Her collection of souvenirs included a pink beach towel, pieces of his tie and records, which he had thrown down from his balcony to the fans, and a blue and white shirt that Elvis had handed her himself.

The headline in the *Honolulu Star Bulletin*, 14 November "Pony-Tail Set Rocks Pier 10 As Idol Elvis Presley Sails Away". The article by Shirley Hutton in the Honolulu Star Bulletin on 15 November was: "Elvis Is Gone, But The Memory - And Troubles -. Linger For No. 1 Fan." In the article she was referring to Barbara Wong, whose hooky playing resulted in disciplinary action by the Director of the Castle High School, Clarence Watson. The punishment by her parents was that she was not allowed to participate in the Castle Kailua High School football game, a very important social event for the students of both schools. "I cannot help me," said Barbara,, "but it was almost as if I was not who did these things. But I did it for Elvis and I would do it again." "It seemed as though her parents could understand her." "It was not right that our girl has skipped school," said her stepfather, James McGinley, "but her mother and I are actually pretty proud that our small, quiet Barbara did all the things she planned to do".

Tour promoter Lee Gordon, who remained a few days after Elvis' departure in Honolulu, told the press that Elvis "really liked it here" and that in his heart he always has a soft spot for Hawaii.

Excerpts from http://elvislightedcan.free-forums.org

Elvis with a fan and his manager aboard the USS Lurline.

Elvis arrived in San Francisco (or Los Angeles). No fans were waiting for him.

 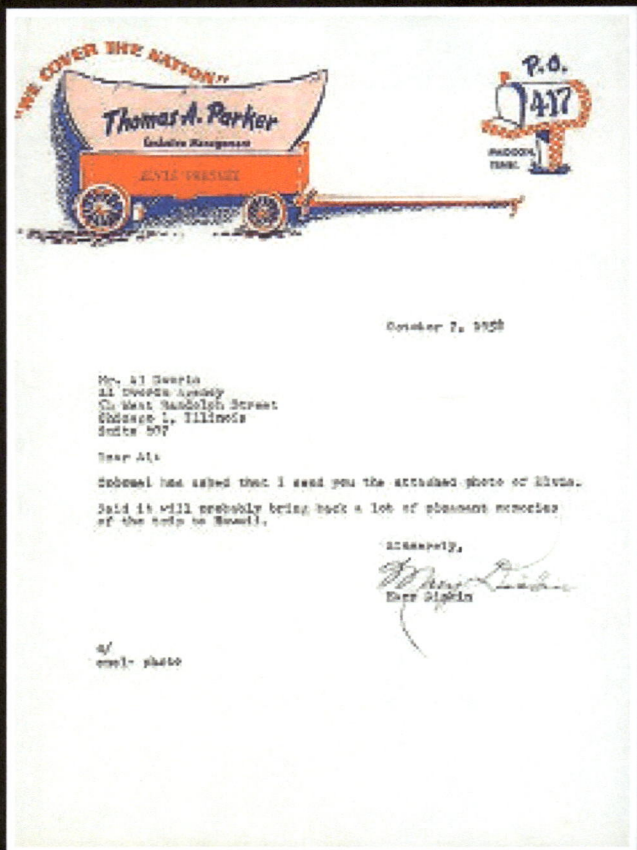

Letter dated October 7, 1958 from Tom Parker to Al Dvorin. It reads:

Dear Al,

Colonel has asked that I send the attached photo of Elvis.

Said it will probably bring back a lot of pleasant memories of the trip to Hawaii.

Top: The statue to commemorate the Elvis concert that was held at the *Neal Blaisdell* arena in 1973.
Below: Fumie Nakao shows the picture that was taken during Elvis' visit in Hawaii in 1957. She is on the far right of the B&W photograph.

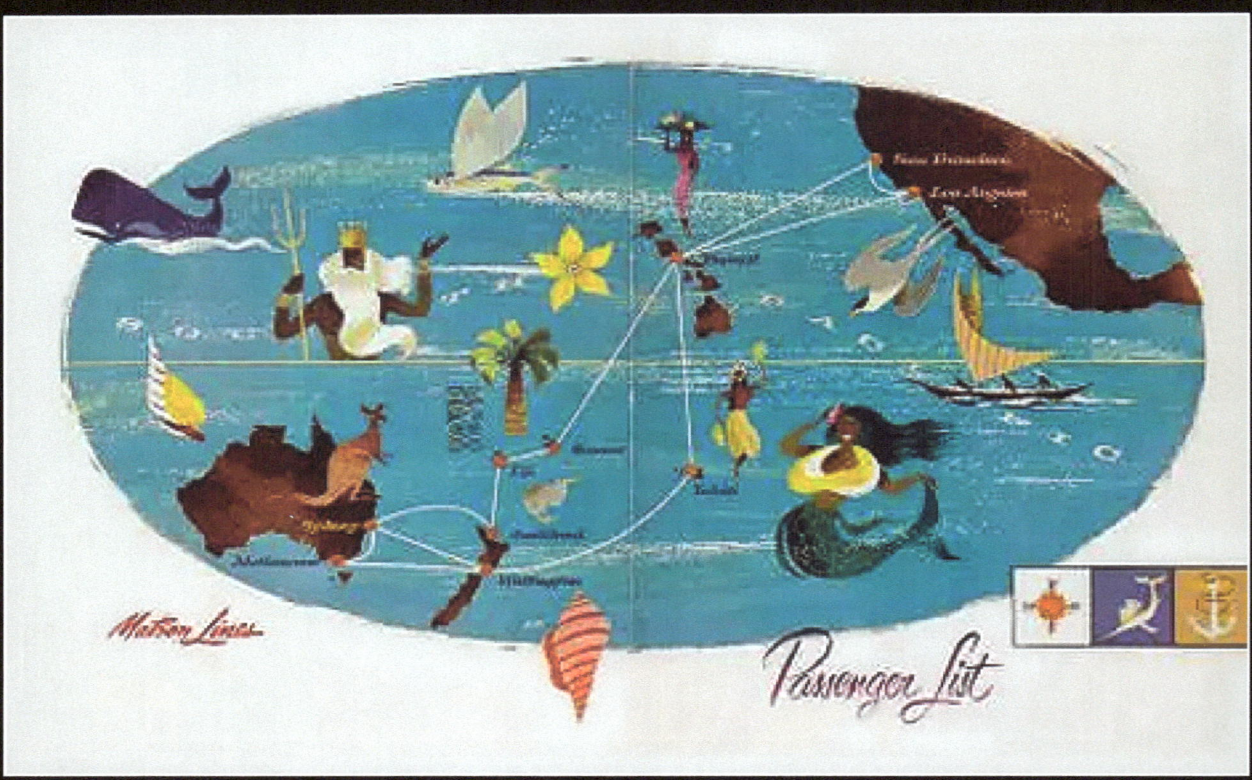

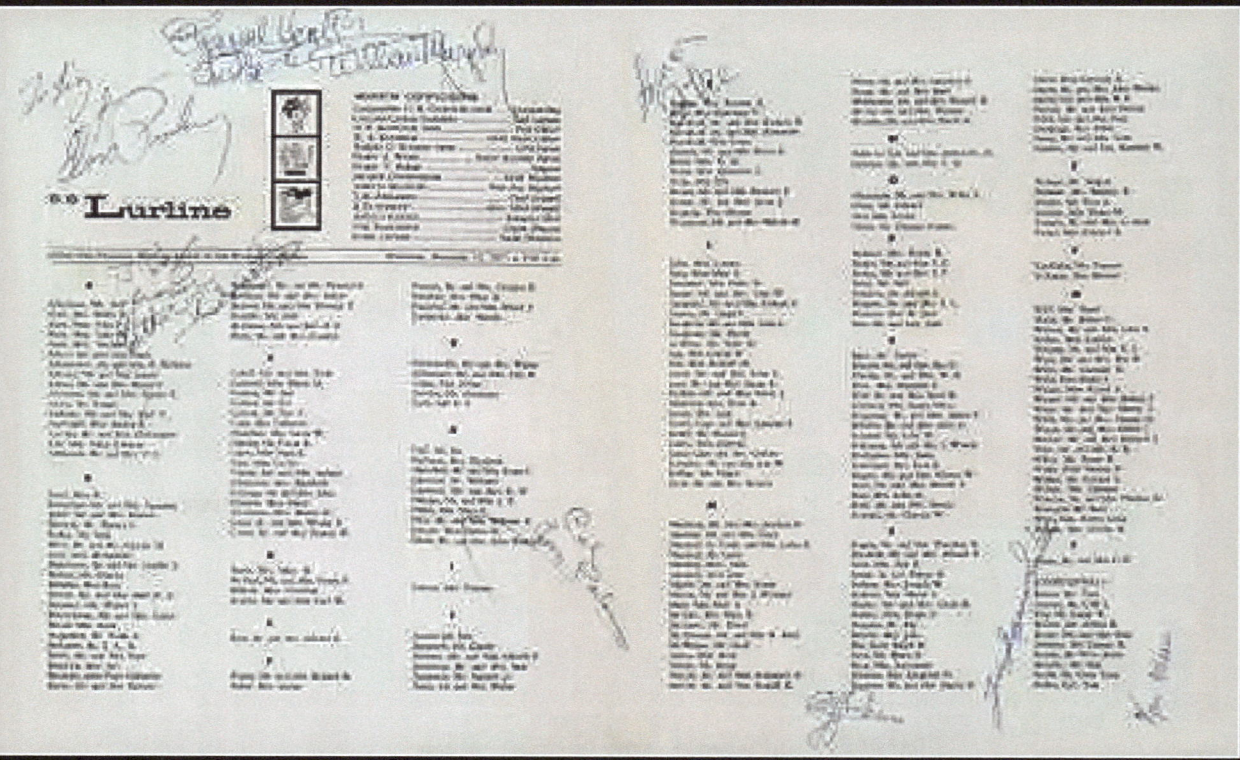

Above is the USS Lurline's passenger list. The Elvis party is listed as "Confidential." It has been autographed by Elvis, Tom Parker, and others such as Mrs. Moore, the wife of Elvis' head of security, Ken Moore. This item sold for $2,600 at auction on August 23, 2014.

Acknowledgments

I am thankful to the Elvis fan clubs all over the world, particularly their websites which were an invaluable resource. A few were consulted regularly, such as The Elvis Information Network at www.elvisinfonet.com, www.elvispresleymusic.com.au, www.elvis-collectors.com, www.elvisechoesofthepast.com, www.elvispresleyphotos.com, www.elvis.com.au, www.scottymoore.net.

I would be remiss if I did not mention all the help I got from the Web, particularly Wikipedia, the free Encyclopedia. It has become an unfailing source of information. Conversely, the information available on the internet is regurgitated so many times that it is extremely difficult to trace the original source of the material, too often at the expense of the originator.

In addition to the sources mentioned above, pictures also appeared on internet sites such as Pinterest, Tumblr and others. Every effort has been made to trace the copyright holders, but it has not always proved feasible. I do however extend our thanks to anyone we may not have been able to contact, and should a specific credit be required, it will appear in any other edition of this book.

I thank my wife Dorothy for her continuous and insightful help during the years of researching and writing this book. Her expertise and recommendations have made this book much better than I had envisioned.

Bibliography

Books:

Honolulu Stadium: Where Hawaii Played, Arthur Suehiro, Watermark Publishing, 1995.
Elvis in Hawaii, Jerry Hopkins, Bess Press, 2002.
The Elvis Files Magazine, December 2013.
Movie Teen's Elvis Yearbook, 1960.
Last Train to Memphis, Peter Guralnick,
Elvis, The Final Fifties Tours, Alan Hanson, iUniverse, 2007.

Websites:

www.elvis-collectors.com
www.scottymoore.net
www.elvispresleymusic.com.au
www.pinterest.com: Sly Mino
www.pinterest.com: Tanja Graf
www.pinterest.com: Sanja Meegin
www.elvisinfonet.com
www.elvislightedcan.free-forums.org
www.elvis.com.au

Videos:

www.youtube.com: 1957 - Elvis in Hawaii - November 10 - Honolulu Stadium
www.youtube.com: Elvis on the way to Hawaii 1957
www.youtube.com: Elvis Presley on ship to Hawaii 1957
www.youtube.com: Elvis Goes Hawaii '57
www.youtube.com: The Ron Jacobs Story - Elvis Comes to Hawaii 1957

www.ingramcontent.com/pod-product-compliance
Lightning Source LLC
Chambersburg PA
CBHW040904020526
44114CB00037B/55